What would it be like to swim in the sea as a killer whale—or a barracuda? How would it feel to be a spotted grouper waiting motionless to ambush your unsuspecting victim?

Prepare to embark on an outrageous journey with the most exciting and dangerous creatures of the sea. From the deepest seas to the barrier reefs, fantastic illustrations will transport you to the remotest and most spectacular marine settings imaginable.

You will marvel over the grotesque, ragged rows of teeth the moray eel uses to capture prey in its giant jaws before swallowing it whole. See the horrifying beauty of the Portuguese man-of-war, with its long slender tentacles covered with stinging cells, waiting to fill its victim with paralyzing venom. You will be stunned by the six-foot-long angler fish that lies perfectly still except for the rod-like lure it dangles over its head until its prey is devoured in a perfectly timed gulp.

More than twenty riveting accounts of the majesty of great predators of the sea.

Also from Tor Books

Great Predators of the Land by Q. L. Pearce

The Stargazer's Guide to the Galaxy by Q. L. Pearce

How Do You Go to the Bathroom in Space? by William R. Pogue
with an Introduction by John Glenn

GREAT
PREDATORS
OF THE
SEA

Q. L. PEARCE
Illustrated by Joe Yakovetic

Reviewed and endorsed by Michael Dee,
Curator of Mammals and Carnivores, Los Angeles Zoo

A Tom Doherty Associates Book
New York

To the students of Cahuilla Elementary School in Palm Springs, California—authors all.

Q.L.P.

GREAT PREDATORS OF THE SEA

Copyright © 1999 by RGA Publishing Group, Inc.

Cover and interior art by Joe Yakovetic
Design by Susan Shankin

This book is printed on acid-free paper.

A Tor Book
Published by Tom Doherty Associates, LLC
175 Fifth Avenue
New York, NY 10010

Tor Books on the World Wide Web:
http://www.tor.com

Tor® is a registered trademark of Tom Doherty Associates, LLC

ISBN 0-312-85979-1

First Edition: July 1999

Printed in the United States of America

0 9 8 7 6 5 4 3 2 1

Contents

Introduction: Predator and Prey

The word "predator" usually brings to mind large, fierce animals that capture and kill other animals. Although this image is certainly accurate, a predator is actually *any* animal that hunts, captures, and kills its own food. The predator's victims, the animals it hunts and kills, are called its prey. Great predators of the sea are not always the largest or strongest animals. Great predators are those hunters that are successful enough to thrive.

The first relationships between predators and prey developed in the warm waters of Earth's seas, and predator-prey relationships have contin-ued in the sea ever since. About 3 billion years ago, the first single-celled organisms drifted in the warm ocean waters. These organisms were the ancestors of all modern animals. Some of the organisms fed upon single-celled plants that used sunlight to produce their own food. Some may also have fed upon miner-als taken directly from the water. Still other organisms probably ate the remains of dead organisms. Although scientists cannot say exactly when, at some point in history certain animal-like organisms developed that were able to capture and feed upon other living organisms. The predator and prey were born.

Modern predators of the sea have developed some remarkable tools and skills for captur-ing and killing prey. These predators may have great strength, sharp teeth, poisonous venom, great speed, or the ability to produce electricity in large amounts. They may also have highly developed or special senses that are extremely sensitive to motion, sounds, light, or smells. Still other predators hunt in groups, trap their prey, or blend in with their surroundings and launch surprise attacks. Most great predators use a combination of tools and skills. Predators usu-ally kill only to survive. They

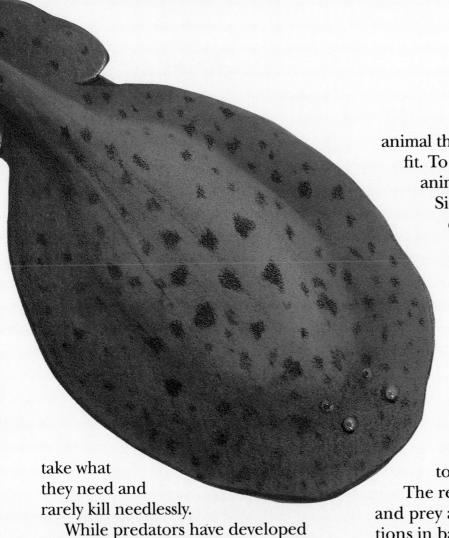

take what
they need and
rarely kill needlessly.

While predators have developed these special tools and skills to capture and kill prey, the prey animals have developed methods to avoid being captured. A prey animal may freeze, flee, hide, or fight when threatened. And just like the predators, the prey animals have also developed a wide range of special tools and skills. They may protect themselves with armor, claws, spines, poison, great size or speed, or just by blending in with their natural surroundings.

Strange as it may seem, the relationship between predator and prey benefits both the animal that is hunting and the animal that is hunted by keeping both fit. To survive in the sea, predatory animals must be in top condition. Sick or injured predators that cannot hunt will not survive. They may even become prey for other, more capable predators. Most of the time, however, even the best and most fit predators are successful in capturing only weak, sick, or old prey animals. This allows the prey species to also stay in top condition, since only the fittest survive to breed.

The relationship between predator and prey also keeps animal populations in balance. If predators did not hunt, there would be little to control the number of prey animals. The prey animals might then use up their own food supply and compete with other animals for food. For example, when people hunted the sea otters of the Southern California coast nearly to extinction, populations of sea urchins, which are animals eaten by sea otters, grew out of control. Sea urchins eat a type of seaweed called kelp that is important as food and shelter for many other species. The sea urchins soon threatened large areas of kelp. Now, the number of sea otters is increasing and the population of sea urchins is slowly dropping as well.

So, as you can see, the predator-prey relationship plays a very important part in the balance of nature.

Traps and Lures

Many predatory animals of the sea are active hunters. They rely on speed or the ability to move skillfully in water to help them capture prey. Predators that are not active hunters need other methods to coax possible victims to within striking distance. One of the ways a predator may do this is to use a trap. Once the trap is set, the predator waits until an unsuspecting animal swims too close and gets caught. Another way a predator that does not actively hunt may capture prey is to use a lure. A lure is a part of the animal's body that attracts the prey close enough so that it can be grabbed in a perfectly timed gulp.

- **The Anglerfish**

- **The Portuguese Man-of-War**

The Anglerfish

Because of its wide, flat head, huge mouth, and warty skin, the anglerfish is sometimes said to be the world's ugliest fish. Although the anglerfish is not attractive, its appearance gives it an advantage over its prey. The anglerfish blends in so well with the rocks and plants on the bottom of the sea that it is nearly impossible for prey animals to see it.

There are many varieties of anglerfish living in tropical and temperate waters throughout the world. Most live in fairly shallow water on the sandy or muddy bottom. The anglerfish usually just lies there motionless and rarely wastes its energy by swimming. The largest anglerfish grow to about 6 feet in length and may weigh as much as 90 pounds.

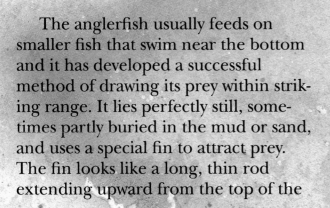

The anglerfish usually feeds on smaller fish that swim near the bottom and it has developed a successful method of drawing its prey within striking range. It lies perfectly still, sometimes partly buried in the mud or sand, and uses a special fin to attract prey. The fin looks like a long, thin rod extending upward from the top of the anglerfish's head. The anglerfish can actively jiggle this rod, which is tipped with a wormlike flap of flesh. The jiggling flap is a lure that attracts other hungry fish. Once the curious victim is close enough, the anglerfish opens its enormously wide mouth and sucks in the fish. The rows of sharp, backward-curving teeth in the anglerfish's mouth make it impossible for the victim to escape. The anglerfish then swallows its prey whole.

The lure: There are about 20 species of anglerfish that swim actively near the bottom of very deep ocean waters. Simply wiggling a lure would do little to attract prey in this dark world, so the fleshy flap that is the deep-sea anglerfish's lure contains bacteria that give off light. The bacteria produce a reddish, yellow-green, or bluish light that attracts other fish. Once a fish that sees this glowing lure swims near, it disappears quickly into the anglerfish's wide mouth.

The Portuguese Man-of-War

The Portuguese man-of-war floats on the surface of all Earth's warm seas. This animal is actually a colony of hundreds of individual animals called polyps. The largest of the polyps is a hollow, gas-filled bag called a float. The float is the only part of the Portuguese man-of-war that can be seen on the surface of the water. It may be as much as 12 inches long and 6 inches high. The top of the float has a high, scalloped crest that varies in color from green to blue to pink to reddish purple. The crest catches the wind and acts like a sail to move the man-of-war along in the water. Hanging down from the float in the water are three other kinds of polyps. Each kind performs a different function. Some polyps trap prey, others feed on the prey, and still others are responsible for reproduction.

The polyps that allow the Portuguese man-of-war to trap prey have long, slender tentacles that are practically invisible to prey animals in the water. These tentacles hang from 20 to 100 feet below the float and are covered with stinging cells. When prey such as fish or shrimp brush up against the tentacles, the stinging cells shoot out into the victim's skin. Venom is injected into the prey and even the most active victim is quickly paralyzed. Then the tentacles contract and move upward, bringing the prey into position for the feeding polyps. The feeding polyps spread over the victim, release digestive juices over it, and then absorb the digested food.

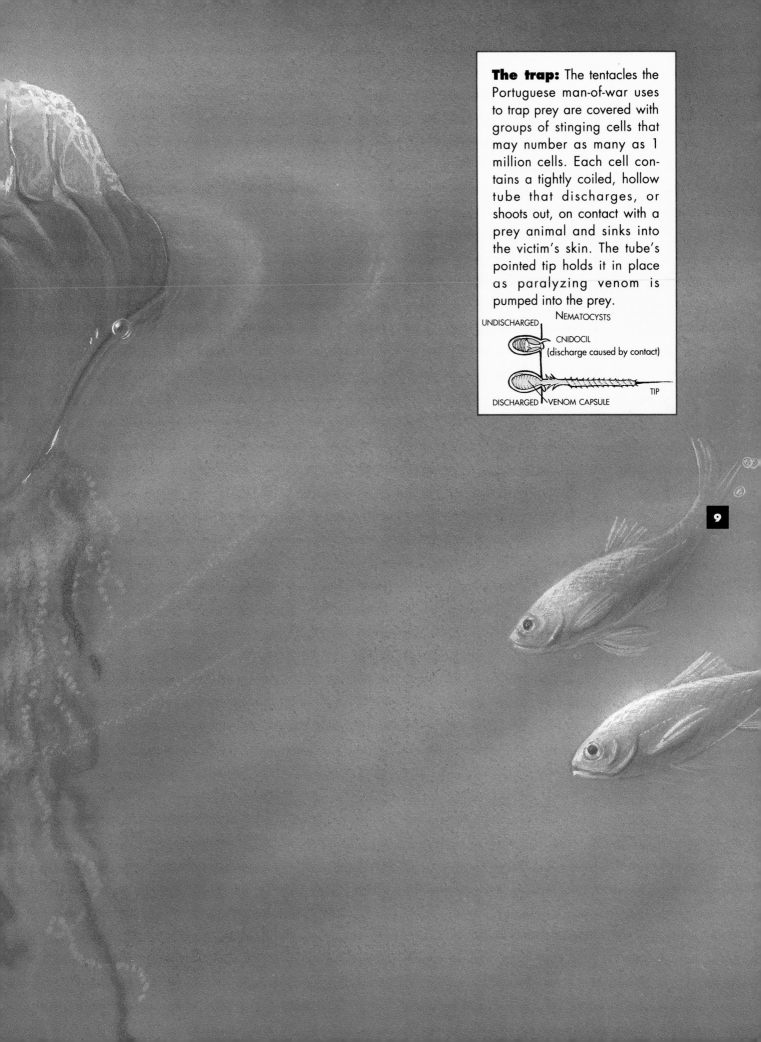

The trap: The tentacles the Portuguese man-of-war uses to trap prey are covered with groups of stinging cells that may number as many as 1 million cells. Each cell contains a tightly coiled, hollow tube that discharges, or shoots out, on contact with a prey animal and sinks into the victim's skin. The tube's pointed tip holds it in place as paralyzing venom is pumped into the prey.

NEMATOCYSTS

UNDISCHARGED

CNIDOCIL
(discharge caused by contact)

DISCHARGED VENOM CAPSULE TIP

9

The Cone Snail

There are more than 400 different species of cone snails, and their cone-shaped shells are often colorfully patterned and very beautiful. Most cone snails are found in the warm waters of the South Pacific Ocean and Indian Ocean. All these snails use venom to kill their prey.

The beautiful but very dangerous 5-inch-long geography cone snail of the South Pacific produces some of

Venom

Some predatory animals rely on deadly venom to injure or kill their prey. Venom is a poisonous substance produced by these animals and introduced into their prey. Because it works quickly and efficiently, venom can help a slow-moving predator to kill an animal that is much faster or stronger than itself. The venom may be delivered into prey by biting, stabbing, or stinging.

- **The Cone Snail**

- **The Octopus**

- **The Sea Snake**

the deadliest venom of all the cone snails. The geography cone spends the day burrowing in the sand. At night, the snail comes out to feed. It uses its powerful venom to paralyze and kill small fish, such as blennies and gobies, that live close to the sandy bottom of the sea. The venom is contained in a sac behind the snail's mouth opening. When a prey animal comes in contact with the geography cone, the snail shoots out a tiny, hollow, barbed "dart" from the end of its snout and into the victim. The dart then releases venom into the prey animal. The victim is paralyzed in as little as a few seconds. The snail then slowly draws the whole fish into its mouth and begins to digest it. If the geography cone snail misses its target, it takes about 10 minutes for the snail to prepare another of its darts for an attack.

11

The dart: The darts of all cone snails are hollow and are made of the same material that forms the outer skeletons of insects. Several darts are stored in a sac in the snail's body. Touching prey causes the venom gland within the snail's body to contract, squeezing out one of the darts as well as the venom. Although the dart usually stays attached to the end of the snail's snout during the capture of prey, each dart is used only once. After it is used, the dart is discarded.

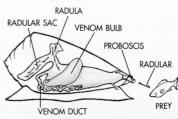

RADULA
RADULAR SAC   VENOM BULB
PROBOSCIS
RADULAR
VENOM DUCT   PREY

The Octopus

Octopuses are found in all the oceans of the world. They are considered to be among the most intelligent of the invertebrates, which are animals without backbones. The octopus is usually shy and likes to keep to itself, but it is well equipped to be a good hunter. The octopus is named for its eight flexible arms (*octo* means "eight" in Latin). It uses one or more of its arms to grab prey, such as fish, crab, or lobster. Each arm is lined with small, round disks. By contracting muscles around each disk, the octopus is able to create a suction force that gives it an excellent grip. The predator then paralyzes its prey with a venomous bite.

There are about 150 species of octopus. The common octopus may grow to be more than 10 feet across its arms, but the tiny blue-ringed octopus of Australia (shown here) has the deadliest venom of all the octopuses. This animal is only 6 inches across its arms, but its venom is powerful enough to kill an adult person. Like other octopuses, however, this tiny hunter keeps to itself and avoids people. At night, it glides out from its hiding place and waits patiently for a likely victim to pass by. When it sees its prey, the octopus creeps to within attack range. Then it suddenly dashes at the victim and traps it in a grip that cannot be escaped.

12

13

The deadly beak: The octopus often eats prey animals that have hard shells, such as the crab, shown below. To crush its victims, the octopus uses its hard, horny beak, which looks like a parrot's beak. When the octopus bites down, venom is released from special glands near the animal's mouth. Venom is not injected into the victim's body. Instead, it may flow through the bite wound, or it may be absorbed by prey animals directly through their gills. Depending on its size, a prey animal is either swallowed whole or torn into bite-sized pieces and then swallowed bit by bit.

VENOM GLAND

BEAK

SIPHON

The Sea Snake

Sea snakes are usually found in the shallow waters of the South Pacific. These reptiles are well suited for life in the water. Their slightly flattened bodies and wide, flat tails help make them excellent swimmers. Sea snakes do not have the broad scales on their bellies that allow land snakes to crawl. Therefore, these snakes are practically helpless on land, and most of them never come ashore. Instead of laying eggs as most land snakes do, sea snakes give birth in the water to living young. Even though the sea snakes live in water, they need air to breathe. They can remain underwater for about an hour, but eventually they must come to the surface for air.

All sea snakes use venom to kill their prey, but the 3-foot-long beaked sea snake shown here has the most deadly venom. Some scientists claim that this snake has the most powerful venom of any snake on land or sea. The beaked sea snake lives in the waters of Southeast Asia. It is colored and patterned to blend in with its surroundings on the shallow sea floor. It waits on the sea floor until a possible victim, such as a small fish, comes along. Then the snake quickly bites the victim with its sharp fangs. Venom is injected into the prey, and within a few moments the victim is dead. The beaked sea snake is able to open its mouth very wide. This allows the predator to bite and swallow even fairly large fish.

The venom: There are three basic types of venom. Cardiotoxic venoms affect the heart directly, hemotoxic venoms affect the blood, and neurotoxic venoms affect the nervous system. As is the case with most venomous animals, the beaked sea snake's venom has elements of all three types, but it is mainly a neurotoxic venom. The venom works on the nerves of an animal and causes it to become paralyzed. This paralysis prevents the victim from breathing and quickly stops its heart from beating.

FANG VENOM GLAND

HEART

NERVE

BLOOD VESSELS

17

The Moray Eel

Ambush and Camouflage

Predatory animals sometimes use ambush, which is a surprise attack from a hiding place, to capture their prey. A predator will often remain hidden or motionless before attacking its victim. A camouflaged hunter, one that is colored or patterned to blend with its surroundings, has an extra advantage as it waits for an unsuspecting victim to wander by. Being able to launch a surprise attack increases the hunter's chances for success.

- **The Moray Eel**

- **The Stonefish**

- **The Spotted Grouper**

18

There are more than one hundred species of moray eels living in tropical and temperate seas around the world. Moray eels are usually found among coral or rocky reefs, and they come in a wide variety of colors and patterns. The moray's scaleless, leathery skin may be green, yellow, or brown. It may also be speckled with colorful spots or striped in black and white like a zebra. Most moray eels are between 5 and 6 feet in length, and some may be 10 feet long or more.

A victim that fights back: One of the moray eel's favorite meals is octopus. Following the octopus's scent, the moray slithers easily into the places where an octopus might hide. When the moray finds its prey, it grips the octopus with its backward-curving teeth. Sometimes an octopus will fight back by clamping its arms around the moray's head. When this happens, the moray may form a loop with its own tail. It draws its body backward through the loop and frees itself from the octopus's headlock.

With its head in the grasp of an octopus, the eel forms a knot in its tail.

It then eases its head backward through the knot.

Finally, the eel frees itself from the octopus's grip.

Despite this size, these predators are often difficult to see in the water because they usually keep about two-thirds of their length hidden in rocky cracks or crevices.

The moray eel hunts actively at night and it relies mainly on its sense of smell to help it locate prey. Moving only slightly with the water, moray eels wait in ambush and watch for passing fish or crabs. When a prey animal comes close enough, it is snapped up and swallowed whole. The moray must swallow the prey animal as quickly as possible. It must do this because to breathe, the moray must constantly draw water into its open mouth, and swallowing interferes with the continuous flow of water. The moray's open mouth makes the animal's sharp, ragged teeth almost always visible, giving the predator a ferocious appearance. For a long time people thought the moray eel had a venomous bite, but its teeth are, in fact, only used to grip prey.

The Stonefish

The stonefish is found in calm waters along the coasts of the Pacific Ocean. It lives among the rocks and coral on the shallow, tropical ocean floor. Without a close inspection, it is almost impossible to tell the stonefish from a large lump of rock. The stonefish, which is 1 to 2 feet long, has a heavy head that is broad and flat. Its mouth is wide and its body is covered with bumps and warts. Some stonefish even have simple forms of seaweed growing here and there on their scaleless skin. To complete the disguise, the stonefish hardly ever moves at all. It rests perfectly still on the shallow floor of the sea, sometimes partly covered by sand. Even the stonefish's breathing does not give away the fish's location. When a fish breathes, water enters the fish's mouth and leaves through its gill slits. The stonefish's gill slits are located so that the water given off during breathing does not disturb the sand.

The stonefish hunts by ambushing its prey. As it rests on the ocean floor, camouflaged to look like a rock, the stonefish is actually waiting for its food to come along. When a prey animal, such as a small fish, draws near, the stonefish goes into action. It launches itself at the victim in a lightning-fast attack and snaps up the animal in the blink of an eye. The stonefish gobbles down its victim whole and then settles back to wait for the next victim to come by.

Venomous spines: The stonefish's extremely poisonous venom is stored in glands at the bottom of 13 hollow spines along the fish's back. The stonefish rests on the bottom of the sea with its spines pointing up. If a person wading in shallow water steps on the sharp spines, venom is injected into the person's foot. Unless a person gets immediate medical treatment, the results can be fatal.

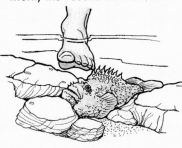

STONEFISH CAMOUFLAGED AMONG ROCKS

The Spotted Grouper

Spotted groupers are found around the world in warm, tropical waters, usually among coral reefs. The smallest groupers are less than a foot long. The largest, such as the Queensland grouper of Australia, may be as long as 12 feet and weigh as much as 800 pounds. It may be hard to imagine how a fish this large can hide, but ambush is the grouper's chief method of obtaining prey.

Spotted groupers hunt mainly during the day. They lurk almost motionless among the rocks and coral in moderately shallow waters. To improve their camouflage, most groupers can change color. These fish have hundreds of tiny color cells in their skin. By opening some of these cells and closing others, groupers can change the overall color or pattern of their skin to better match their background. One grouper, the Nassau grouper, has at least eight different color stages. This fish may be all dark, all white, dark and white, speckled, banded, or a variety of other colors and patterns.

When a prey fish swims within range, the well-hidden spotted grouper opens its huge mouth and sucks in the victim. The grouper uses its strong jaws lined with sharp, spiky, backward-pointing teeth to hold the struggling animal. Once the victim is firmly in the grouper's grasp, the huge predatory fish swallows its prey whole.

An irresistible force:

The spotted grouper draws in its prey by first raising the flaps of skin that cover the gills on either side of its head. Raising the gill covers draws a great amount of water into the fish's huge mouth. Along with the water, the grouper sucks in its startled victim. The water is then let out through the predator's gill openings as the victim is swallowed. This entire swallowing process takes only a fraction of a second.

PREY

The grouper sucks in prey with water.

As water exits the gills, the prey is captured in the mouth.

23

The Mako Shark

Mako sharks live in the warm, deep waters of the tropical and temperate open ocean. They usually grow to about 6 feet long, but some makos may reach 12 feet in length and weigh 1200 pounds. These great predators can swim through the water at more than 50 miles per hour.

Everything about the mako shark is built for speed. Its pointed snout and torpedo-shaped body help

Speed

Predatory animals capable of great speed are often the most successful hunters. The predator that can quickly close the distance between itself and its victim has a good chance of capturing its prey. Of course, many prey animals manage to escape capture by fleeing quickly. So the hungry predator must be especially speedy, alert, and quick in the water in order to surprise and capture its prey.

- **The Mako Shark**

- **The Sailfish**

reduce water resistance by allowing the mako to move quickly through the water as it swims. The shark's rigid fins provide balance and steadiness when swimming at high speeds. The mako's spine continues into its tail, giving it extra power and support when swimming.

The mako eats a wide variety of fish and swallows small animals whole. However, it often goes after more challenging prey. The mako shark readily attacks some of the largest, fastest fish in the sea, including tuna and swordfish. The mako will swim after its victim in a high-speed chase until it is close enough to nip off the victim's tail with its slender, widely spaced teeth. Without a tail, the victim can no longer swim away. The mako is then able to tear off chunks of flesh and swallow its prey bite by bite.

Skin teeth: Sharks do not have scales like most other fish. Instead, their skin is covered by special toothlike scales called denticles. In the mako shark, these tiny, tough "skin teeth" are designed to help the mako move easily through the water. The denticles have grooved surfaces and slightly raised, mushroom shapes that allow water to pass smoothly over the mako's skin. This lessens water resistance and adds to the mako shark's ability to swim swiftly.

Water flows easily past denticles.

SKIN   DENTICLE

The Sailfish

The sailfish is found in all warm, tropical waters and is one of the fastest fish in the sea. It may reach a speed of almost 70 miles per hour, which is more than three times as fast as the fastest person can run in a short race. The sailfish has a slender body that is usually 7 to 8 feet long and weighs less than 300 pounds. At least 2 feet of the sailfish's length are taken up by its upper jaw, which is actually a sharp, pointed, swordlike bill. Some scientists believe the bill is used mainly to slash at prey. Other scientists suggest the bill's main purpose is to cut through the water, thus reducing water resistance.

The sailfish's body is designed for traveling at great speed. When chasing after a meal of fish, the torpedo-shaped sailfish propels itself with its strong, muscular tail. Its gills have a large surface area. A great deal of water is able to pass over this large area, which increases the amount of oxygen available to the fish. This helps supply the sailfish with the oxygen it needs to swim at high speed.

When the hunting sailfish finds a group of small fish, it may swim rapidly in tight circles around the fish. This swift circling drives the fish into a small, tight group. Then the sailfish charges speedily through the group of prey, thrashing its long, sharp bill from side to side and killing or stunning large numbers of fish. The toothless sailfish then swallows its prey whole.

Fabulous fin: One of the most noticeable features of the sailfish is its large dorsal, or back, fin. The fish is actually named for this fin, which looks like a sail. The fin may be as high as 3 feet and stretch for half the length of the fish. The purpose of this unusual fin is not certain. During high-speed swimming, the sailfish folds down its dorsal fin into a groove along its back. When the sailfish is circling around groups of prey, its fin is often half raised. The sailfish has also been seen drifting calmly at the surface of the water with its fin fully raised.

The Bluefish

The bluefish is one of the most ferocious killers in the warm and temperate waters of the Atlantic Ocean and Indian Ocean. It seems to have an unending appetite for all kinds of fish. Usually, bluefish are about 1½ to 2 feet long and weigh about 10 pounds, but the largest bluefish on record was 4 feet long and weighed nearly 40 pounds. The bluefish is fast and quick-moving.

Groups

Some predatory animals travel and hunt together in groups. In the sea, these groups are called schools or pods. By cooperating, a group of predators may simply overpower its prey. Or the group may attack its prey from all sides, which frightens the victims and causes them to exhaust themselves trying to escape. Or the group may confuse its prey by cutting off the victims' escape route. When they hunt in large groups, even small predators can overcome large prey.

- **The Bluefish**

- **The Killer Whale**

Bluefish are most well known and dreaded by people who fish in the deep waters off the Atlantic coast of North America. They are dreaded because after a group of bluefish moves through an area, there are few fish left to catch. Bluefish travel and hunt in huge groups called schools. In 1901, a school of bluefish was sighted that stretched over 5 miles of ocean! The hunting methods of bluefish are simple. They swim as a group directly into schools of other fish such as herring and mackerel. Then the bluefish use their sharp teeth to rip apart every fish within reach. They gobble down what they can and then move on, leaving behind a trail of dying fish and parts of dead fish they have not eaten. Because they are so ferocious and rip their victims to pieces, bluefish can eat prey much larger than themselves.

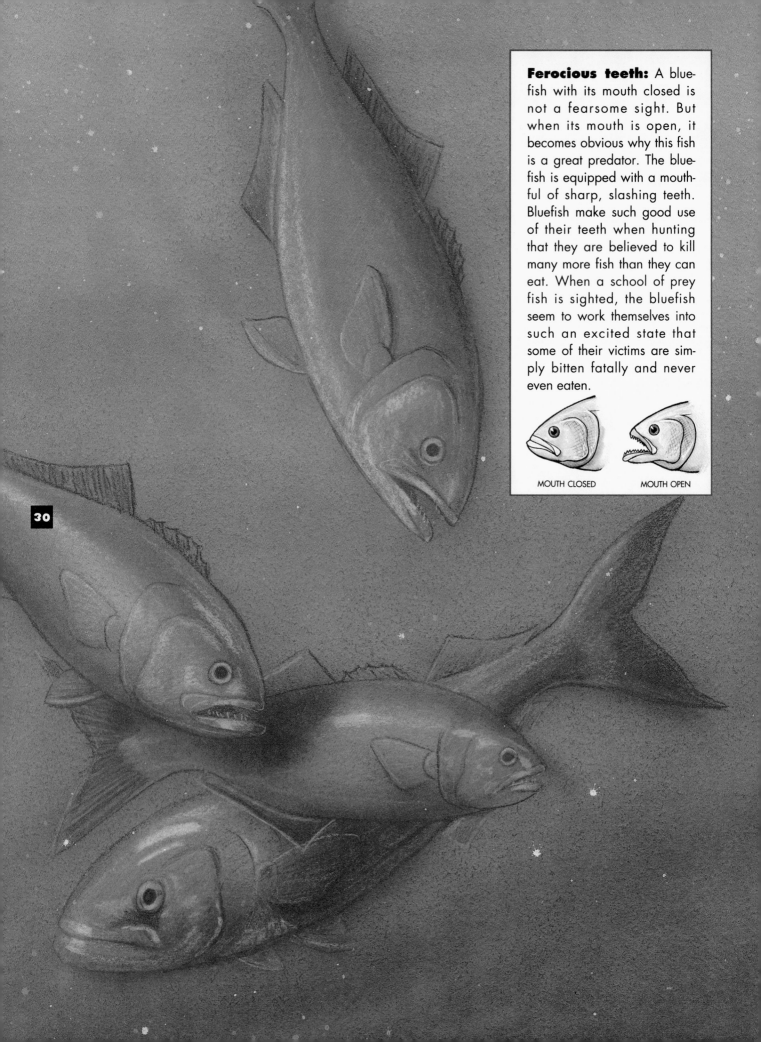

Ferocious teeth: A bluefish with its mouth closed is not a fearsome sight. But when its mouth is open, it becomes obvious why this fish is a great predator. The bluefish is equipped with a mouthful of sharp, slashing teeth. Bluefish make such good use of their teeth when hunting that they are believed to kill many more fish than they can eat. When a school of prey fish is sighted, the bluefish seem to work themselves into such an excited state that some of their victims are simply bitten fatally and never even eaten.

MOUTH CLOSED   MOUTH OPEN

The Killer Whale

Killer whales are found from pole to pole in all the oceans on Earth. This intelligent animal is the largest and most powerful member of the dolphin family. Fully grown males may reach 30 feet in length and may weigh 8 tons. The killer whale is known to feed on almost anything that swims in the sea, including seals, whales, walrus pups, other dolphins, and even polar bears out swimming in search of food. It also eats turtles, sharks, squid, and up to 400 pounds of small fish every day. Although the killer whale swallows small animals whole, this predator has between 40 and 48 sturdy, cone-shaped teeth. These large, heavy, backward-curving

teeth are not used for chewing. Instead, the killer whale uses its teeth to grip prey and to tear chunks of flesh from its bigger victims.

Killer whales hunt and feed in groups called pods. A pod consists of 3 to 40 individuals or more. The pod may travel up to 70 miles a day in search of victims. Killer whales are well equipped to find prey and often use only their eyesight to locate victims. They have excellent vision both in and out of water. Killer whales also use their swimming ability when hunting. During a chase, killer whales can reach speeds of up to 35 miles per hour, which is about nine times faster than the fastest person can swim.

Working together: Killer whales work cooperatively and form well-organized hunts. Once a victim is found, the entire pod may work together to trap prey, such as a shark or small whale. The killer whales begin their attack by forming a circle around the victim. Then they move closer to the animal, trying to slow it down or drown it. Finally, following the lead of one of the males, the entire pod moves in for the kill. The pod then shares its meal. Large chunks are torn from the prey and gulped down.

The Common Dolphin

Special Senses

Predatory animals' senses are among their most important hunting tools. If a predator cannot locate its prey, it has little chance of catching and killing it. Some hunters have highly developed senses of sight, hearing, or smell. A few predators of the sea have developed some surprising sensory skills, such as the ability to detect the electricity produced by other animals. Some predatory animals even produce and use their own electricity to locate prey.

- **The Common Dolphin**

- **The Torpedo Ray**

- **The Bull Shark**

The common dolphin is a torpedo-shaped predator of the deep sea. It is found in all of the world's tropical and temperate oceans and feeds on fish and squid. The common dolphin grows to be up to 8 feet long and may weigh as much as 175 pounds.

The common dolphin rarely comes close to shore. Out in the open ocean, the dolphin uses sound waves to find its prey. As it swims, the dolphin sends out sounds in a series of clicks. The sound waves bounce off nearby objects and the dolphin listens for the returning echoes. Differences in the echoes let the dolphin know whether there are rocks, plants, or a group of tasty fish ahead. This use of sound to locate prey is called echolocation.

When hunting, the common dolphin may dive as deep as 1000 feet, although average dives are closer to 150 feet deep. But since the dolphin needs air to breathe, it does not stay underwater for more than a few minutes. The dolphin usually feeds near the surface of the water, and it has even been seen leaping out of the water to capture flying fish in midair. After the dolphin catches its victim between jaws lined with up to 200 sharp, cone-shaped teeth, it swallows the prey whole.

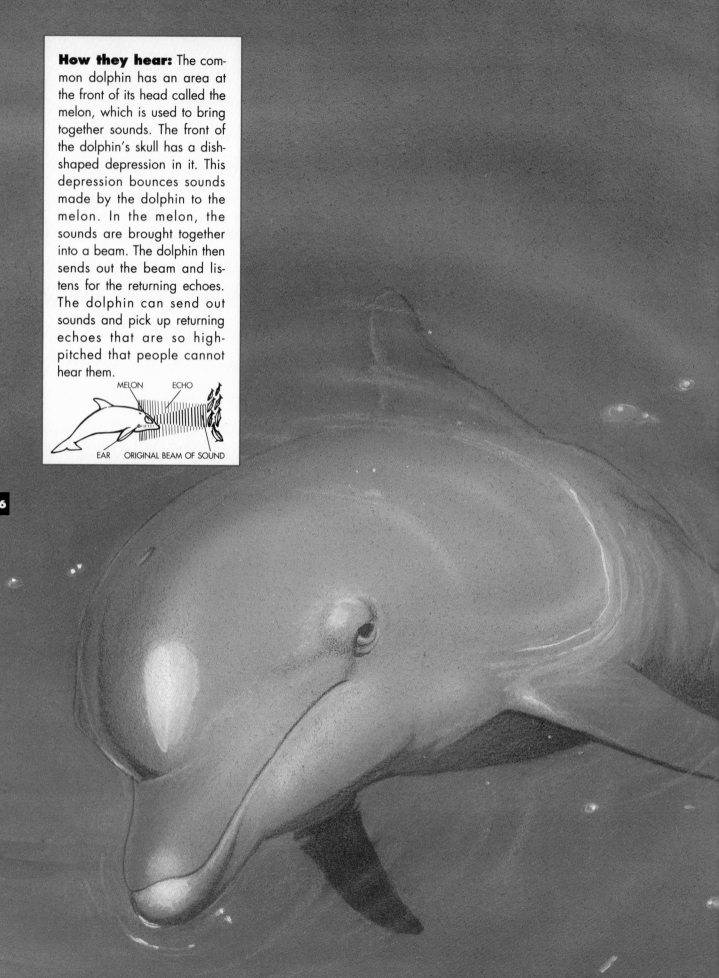

How they hear: The common dolphin has an area at the front of its head called the melon, which is used to bring together sounds. The front of the dolphin's skull has a dish-shaped depression in it. This depression bounces sounds made by the dolphin to the melon. In the melon, the sounds are brought together into a beam. The dolphin then sends out the beam and listens for the returning echoes. The dolphin can send out sounds and pick up returning echoes that are so high-pitched that people cannot hear them.

MELON   ECHO

EAR   ORIGINAL BEAM OF SOUND

The Torpedo Ray

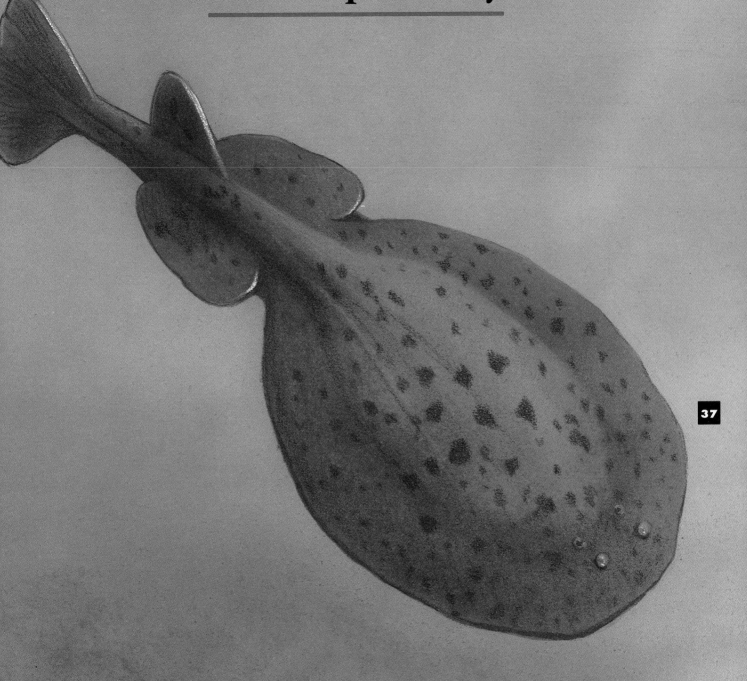

The torpedo ray is a flat, disk-shaped fish that lives in all warm and temperate seas. There are about 30 species of torpedo ray, and they range in length from about 20 inches to 5 feet. All torpedo rays produce electricity at high levels. The electric jolts generated by these rays can pack a wallop of about 200 volts, which is enough to stun or kill a fairly large fish. The torpedo ray uses this ability to produce electricity to capture prey and defend itself. The ray rests partly buried in mud or sand on the bottom of the sea. When a fish swims by, the ray pounces on it. Then the ray wraps its wide, flat fins around the victim and electrocutes it. Once the prey has been stunned, the torpedo ray slowly eats its meal, plucking at the victim's flesh with its tiny, sharp teeth.

The torpedo ray also has a small electric organ in its tail that does not seem to play a part in capturing prey or self-defense. The ray probably uses this organ when exploring its environment. The ray surrounds itself with a weak electrical field that is sensitive to objects in the animal's path or disturbances in the water. This allows the ray to get a "sensory picture" of its surroundings. This ability to "see" or "feel" objects, even in dark, murky water, is called electrolocation.

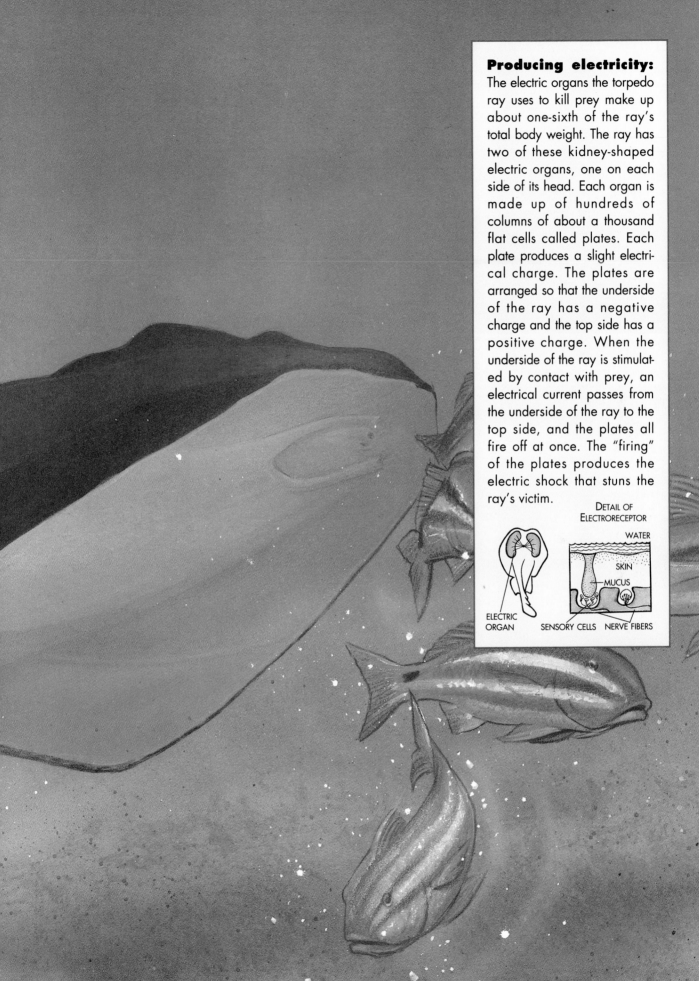

Producing electricity:
The electric organs the torpedo ray uses to kill prey make up about one-sixth of the ray's total body weight. The ray has two of these kidney-shaped electric organs, one on each side of its head. Each organ is made up of hundreds of columns of about a thousand flat cells called plates. Each plate produces a slight electrical charge. The plates are arranged so that the underside of the ray has a negative charge and the top side has a positive charge. When the underside of the ray is stimulated by contact with prey, an electrical current passes from the underside of the ray to the top side, and the plates all fire off at once. The "firing" of the plates produces the electric shock that stuns the ray's victim.

DETAIL OF
ELECTRORECEPTOR

WATER

SKIN

MUCUS

ELECTRIC
ORGAN

SENSORY CELLS   NERVE FIBERS

The Bull Shark

Although the bull shark is found in both the Atlantic Ocean and Pacific Ocean, it is also frequently found in shallow fresh water, such as bays and lakes. There is a large population of bull sharks in Lake Nicaragua in Central America. Even though the lake is 100 miles inland, it is connected to the Caribbean Sea by the San Juan River.

The bull shark has many highly developed senses that help it locate and capture prey. It has an incredible sense of smell and can detect the faint scent of live prey well beyond the distance it can see. The bull shark can even detect the smell of blood from an injured prey animal. Once the bull shark picks up the scent of a possible victim, it follows the trail by moving its broad, rounded snout side to side, all the while closing in on the scent. When at close range, even in dark, murky water, the shark may rely partly on sight. The bull shark's eyes are 10 times more sensitive to light than a person's eyes. The shark can also detect sounds that are higher and lower than people can hear. Amazingly, the bull shark can also "feel" sound. Along its sides are a series of fluid-filled canals known as the lateral lines. The lateral lines are connected to nerves that are sensitive to sound waves and disturbances in the water caused by the movements of prey.

The bull shark is not very particular about what it eats, but it seems to prefer fish and the young of other sharks, such as the sandbar shark.

Detecting electricity:

All animals produce a slight electrical charge in their muscles and nerves when they move and breathe. The bull shark can detect these electrical charges because it has a special network of jelly-filled tubes below the surface of its skin, mainly around the head. Each tube ends in a tiny pit in the shark's skin. The jelly-filled tubes can pick up electrical signals from animals up to 3 feet away. This allows the shark to locate nearby prey even in very dark, murky water.

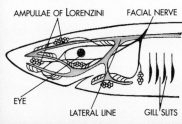

AMPULLAE OF LORENZINI   FACIAL NERVE

EYE

LATERAL LINE   GILL SLITS

Teeth

A predatory animal with a mouthful of sharp teeth has one of the most useful tools for successful hunting. Especially in the sea, where a predator needs a good grip on its slippery victim, powerful teeth and strong jaws are important for holding on to prey until it can be swallowed. The teeth of some predators are used mainly for gripping struggling prey, while the teeth of others are used to slice prey into chunks.

• **The Leopard Seal**

• **The Tiger Shark**

• **The Barracuda**

The Leopard Seal

Like the leopard of Africa and Asia, the leopard seal sports dark spots on a pale coat. The female leopard seal is slightly larger than the male. She may grow to be almost 13 feet long and weigh almost 1000 pounds. The huge leopard seal is an excellent hunter. This predator roams the waters of the Antarctic Ocean searching for a likely victim. In its search for prey, the seal may even travel as far north as the southern coasts of Australia, South Africa, and South America.

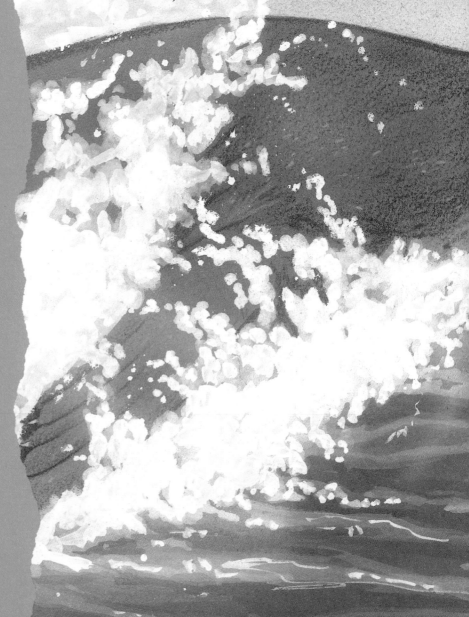

The leopard seal regularly preys on penguins, fish, and squid. It also sometimes attacks young elephant seals and seabirds. When hunting its favorite prey of penguins, the leopard seal may lie in wait near the penguins' breeding grounds. When the penguins come into the water to feed, the leopard seal chases after them. Although the penguins are extremely swift swimmers, the leopard seal is even speedier. When it catches up to a penguin, the seal grabs the victim in its jaws.

The leopard seal has more than one way to kill a penguin. If it spots a penguin in the water, the leopard seal may dive beneath it and swim upward, bumping the victim so soundly from below that it is flung high into the air. The penguin is often already dead from the impact of the blow when it falls back into the water. However, if the penguin escapes the seal and makes it to the shore, it is safe. The leopard seal is clumsy out of water and will not continue the chase on land.

43

Stabbing teeth: The jaws of the leopard seal are lined with large, backward-curving, stabbing teeth that are used to grasp a victim. The seal's jaws also open exceptionally wide, and it has a very stretchy throat. Both of these things allow the seal to easily swallow rather large prey.

The Tiger Shark

Although shark attacks on people are rare, the tiger shark is known to have made more fatal attacks on people than any other kind of shark. Part of the danger is that this shark lives in warm waters where it may come into contact with people who are swimming. The tiger shark usually stays in the deep water at the outer edges of reefs, but it will also enter shallow water. It will eat anything it can swallow, including fish, turtles, seals, smaller sharks, and other objects that happen to be floating by. The list of unusual items recovered from the bellies of tiger sharks includes bottles, cans, shoes, tires, and even an entire chicken coop!

Overpowering its prey is no problem for the tiger shark. This large fish averages between 10 and 15 feet in length and weighs about 1200 pounds, although giant sharks 23 feet long have been reported. The tiger shark hunts alone. It is quick and powerful and may swim up to 50 miles a day looking for prey. This shark also has a muscular tail that can provide an extra burst of speed when the shark is charging at prey. Because of its tall back fin and wedge-shaped head, the tiger shark can also turn quickly when chasing prey. Once a tiger shark has captured its victim in its jaws, it may swallow the animal whole or bite off large chunks with its teeth. The tiger shark's teeth are 2-inch-long, jagged-edged triangles that end in daggerlike points. They are an excellent tool for killing and tearing apart even large prey. Teeth are so important to this predator that even newborn tiger sharks have a full set of teeth and are prepared to hunt immediately after birth.

Replaceable teeth:
The tiger shark's teeth are not firmly fixed in its jaws. Instead, the teeth are held loosely in a tough layer of tissue stretched over the jaws. New teeth grow in quickly to replace those that are lost or broken. These teeth are arranged in replacement rows behind the front row. They develop from tooth buds in a groove inside the shark's jaw. The developing teeth eventually move to the outside edge of the jaw and are replaced by more tooth buds behind them.

RESERVE TEETH ("BUDS") BENEATH SKIN'S SURFACE

TONGUE

The Barracuda

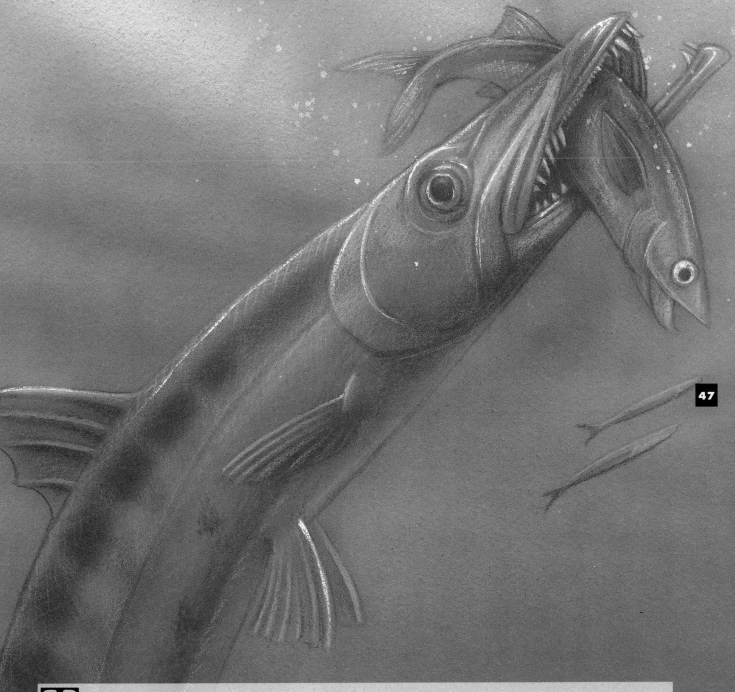

There are about 20 different species of barracudas living in the world's warm oceans and seas. Most barracudas are about 1 to 2 feet long. The largest, however, is the great barracuda, which is found mainly off the southern coast of Florida and in the Caribbean Sea. This huge fish can grow to be 6 to 8 feet long and can weigh about 100 pounds. Large or adult barracudas are usually found in deeper water and they hunt alone. Small, young barracudas are usually found in shallow water, and they hunt in groups called schools.

The barracuda is one of the fiercest

Killer teeth: The barracuda has a large mouth filled with evil-looking teeth. Two sets of teeth line the barracuda's upper jaw. Another two sets line the lower jaw, which juts out beyond the upper jaw. The small, razor-sharp outer teeth are perfect for slashing at a victim. The larger, inner row of teeth are used for gripping and tearing apart prey.

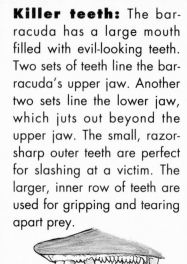

and most dangerous predators of the sea. It has a tremendous appetite and will eat a variety of fish, such as grouper, snapper, and even its own young. It has also been known to snap up seabirds that are resting on the surface of the water.

The barracuda hunts during the day and uses sight, rather than smell, to locate prey. The body of the barracuda is long and slender, allowing it to approach prey slowly and then rocket through the water with great speed and accuracy. Once the decision to attack a fish has been made, the barracuda rushes toward its prey at speeds of up to 27 miles per hour. The barracuda grabs the prey in its front teeth and will swallow the fish whole if it is small. If the prey is large, the barracuda snaps the fish in two with a swift, clean bite. Then it returns to eat the pieces.

When predatory schools of barracudas hunt, they sometimes herd together a group of prey fish. The barracudas then swim around the outside of the group of fish, darting in and out and devouring one or two fish at a time. After eating their fill, the barracudas may herd the remaining fish into shallow water and keep them in sight until they are hungry again.

The Elephant Seal

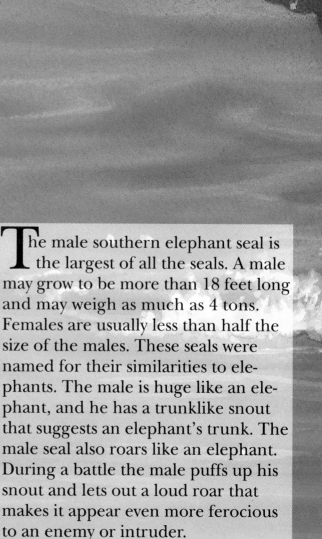

Size and Strength

Large size and great strength are very helpful to predatory animals when they hunt. These traits allow the predators to overpower prey. Great size and strength also make it easier for these animals to protect themselves by fighting off attacks by their enemies. In fact, the biggest, strongest animals often have few natural enemies. Only by developing special weapons or by hunting in groups are smaller, weaker animals able to kill animals larger and stronger than themselves.

- **The Elephant Seal**

- **The Sperm Whale**

- **The Great White Shark**

The male southern elephant seal is the largest of all the seals. A male may grow to be more than 18 feet long and may weigh as much as 4 tons. Females are usually less than half the size of the males. These seals were named for their similarities to elephants. The male is huge like an elephant, and he has a trunklike snout that suggests an elephant's trunk. The male seal also roars like an elephant. During a battle the male puffs up his snout and lets out a loud roar that makes it appear even more ferocious to an enemy or intruder.

Southern elephant seals live mainly in the waters of the Antarctic Ocean. They spend more than 90 percent of their time underwater, feeding on slow-moving fish, sharks, and rays that live deep in the water. In order to reach its prey, the seal must make deep dives to the bottom of the ocean. The females are the better divers, and dives as deep as 4100 feet have been recorded. When hunting, the elephant seal may make two or three dives per hour, staying at the surface of the water for only a few minutes between dives.

The southern elephant seal has a variety of diving styles. In one type of dive, the seal goes down at an angle and then skims along the bottom of the sea searching for prey. Males often look for prey while swimming across the tops of underwater mountains, while females look for prey in deeper water. A single dive may last as long as 45 minutes. To help it dive deep and stay underwater for such a long time, the southern elephant seal has an enormous blood supply with a tremendous number of red blood cells for carrying oxygen.

The Sperm Whale

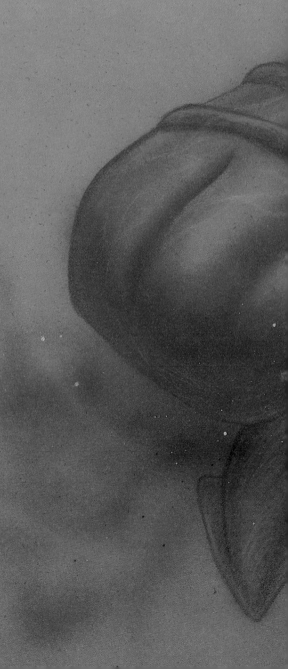

The huge sperm whale, which is found in all the oceans on Earth, is well suited for life in the sea. A layer of blubber, or fat, below its thick skin keeps the whale warm. Glands below the skin produce a fine oil that makes the whale's skin slippery and allows it to glide easily through the water. In addition, the whale's nostrils, or blow-hole, are on top of its head, so the whale only needs to break through the surface of the water to take in air.

The sperm whale hunts deep in the ocean and feeds mostly on octopus and giant squid. It will also eat sharks and other large fish. It is dark at the bottom of the ocean and the sperm whale has poor eyesight, so it uses sounds and echoes to locate prey. Once a victim is located, the whale seizes the prey. The predator uses its cone-shaped teeth to hold on to the animal, which it then swallows whole. But sometimes the victim tries to fight the whale. Because of its size and strength, the whale usually wins the battle. Sperm whales often have scars from battles with their prey.

Because the sperm whale hunts deep in the ocean, it is one of the world's diving champions. Many whales dive as deep as 3000 feet, and dives as deep as 10,000 feet have been reported. To prepare for a dive, the sperm whale first comes to the surface and breathes very quickly a few times. After filling its huge lungs with air, the whale lifts its tail upward and then dives straight down at about 550 feet per minute. The whale may hunt underwater for 45 minutes or longer before returning to the surface.

Majestic size: The sperm whale is the largest of the toothed whales and is easily larger than all the sharks. Adult males are usually 50 to 60 feet long and weigh about 40 tons. The whale's blunt head makes up about a third of its length. Its 50 cone-shaped teeth, each between 6 and 10 inches long, are the largest of any animal. These teeth line only the lower jaw and they fit perfectly into sockets in the upper jaw.

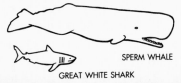

SPERM WHALE

GREAT WHITE SHARK

The Great White Shark

The great white shark is among the biggest and most ferocious fish in the sea. It lives in the open sea in all warm, tropical areas. It may spend time at the surface of the water with its back fin sticking out, but it can also dive as much as a half mile deep. The great white shark swims at about 2 miles per hour, but it may reach a speed of 40 miles per hour in a very short dash. The greatest threat to this huge fish is other, larger great white sharks.

The strong, fearless great white swims through the water eating anything it can catch. Its prey include turtles, tuna, the speedy marlin, and swordfish, as well as dolphins and seals. The great white shark swallows small prey whole. When attacking large animals, the shark opens its huge mouth, exposing a set of 2- to 3-inch-long, triangular, jagged-edged teeth. In the last seconds before an attack, a thin layer of tissue slides up to protect the shark's eyes from injury. Then the shark grabs its prey in its jaws and uses its cutting teeth to slice through the victim. At the same time, the shark shakes its head from side to side to help rip away a huge chunk of flesh and bone from the prey. These chunks are then swallowed and digested.

A huge predator: The great white shark (shown here next to the bull shark) is one of the largest sharks in the sea. The great white averages 10 to 15 feet in length, but it may grow much longer. One great white shark captured off the coast of Australia more than a hundred years ago reportedly measured 36 feet, but its weight is not known and its length was never verified. However, accurate records report that a 21-foot great white shark was caught off Australia with a rod and reel. It weighed nearly 3000 pounds!

GREAT WHITE SHARK

BULL SHARK

Index